CONTENTS

DEAD MEAT!

All animals must eat to survive. Some animal **diets** seem strange. Others are just plain disgusting! **Carcasses** are a part of many animal diets. Animals that eat carcasses are called **scavengers**.

diet what an animal eats
carcass dead body of an animal
scavenger animal that feeds on animals that are already dead

Eating dead animals may
seem horrible. But scavengers are
important. They help to keep the
world clean by removing dead
carcasses. Without scavengers,
dead animals would lie around for
a long time.

Hungry Birds

Vultures dine on dead animals. They also kill sick or dying animals. A group of vultures circle the sky looking for a meal below. Their sharp sense of smell and keen eyesight guide them to their food.

Vultures are made for disgusting
dining. They have bald heads and mostly
bare necks. Too many feathers would get
messy when chewing up a carcass!

Fact!

When they feel threatened, vultures vomit to make their bodies lighter. Then they can fly away more easily.

ROADKILL FOR CROWS

Like many scavengers, crows are **omnivores**. They munch on foods such as meat, fruit and nuts. It's not unusual to see crows on the side of the road. Why? They enjoy feasting on roadkill!

Fact!
Crows also eat insects, snakes, frogs and mice.

omnivore animal that eats plants and other animals

Fact!

Hyenas don't leave much behind.
They even eat bones and hooves!

RUDE HYENAS

Hyenas wait around to eat the leftovers of larger **predators**. Sometimes hyenas boldly steal meals before other animals have finished eating. Hyenas are also fierce predators. They hunt when there are no carcasses near by.

predator animal that hunts other animals for food

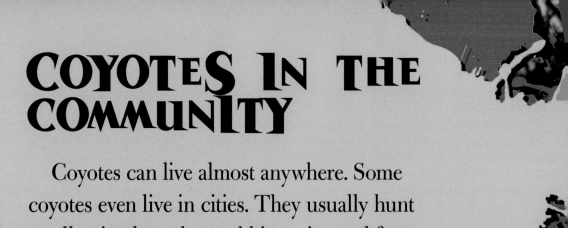

COYOTES IN THE COMMUNITY

Coyotes can live almost anywhere. Some coyotes even live in cities. They usually hunt small animals such as rabbits, mice and frogs. But if they find a dead animal, they will eat that too. Coyotes don't walk away from a free meal!

SLIMY, GOOEY GULPERS

Hagfish are slimy fish that look like eels. Hagfish crawl inside a dead or dying fish on the sea floor. Then they feast on the fish from the inside out.

Fact!
A hagfish's tongue is covered with teeth.

19

CRABBY SNACKS

A lot of dead plants and animals drift down to the bottom of the sea. Crabs are waiting! They scurry around picking up scraps. Crabs keep the sea floor clean.

Fact!
The Japanese spider crab is the world's largest crab. It can reach up to 3.8 metres (12 feet) wide.

SHOO, FLY!

Blowflies lay their eggs on carcasses. When the **larvae** hatch, they feed on the **carrion**. Adult blowflies also nibble on carcasses. They dine on rotting meat, rubbish and animal waste.

Fact!

Adult blowflies also eat **nectar**, but only from stinky flowers. One of their favourites is a flower that smells like rotting meat.

blowfly
larvae

larva insect at the stage of development
between an egg and an adult
carrion flesh of a dead animal
nectar sweet liquid found in many flowers

Fact!
Burying beetles find carcasses by smelling for them with their antennae.

BODYSNATCHING BEETLES

Burying beetles drag small dead **mammals** to their burrows. A female lays her eggs inside the carcass. Then the beetles bury the carcass in the earth. When the larvae hatch, they live inside of and eat the carcass.

mammal animal with hair or fur that gives birth to young and feeds them milk

WORM FOOD

Nothing goes to waste in nature. Earthworms feed on tiny scraps left behind by larger scavengers. Earthworms do more than getting rid of carcasses. Their waste contains **nutrients** that **fertilize** soil.

nutrient parts of food, such as vitamins, that are used for growth
fertilize make soil rich and healthy

TINY BUT MIGHTY

Tiny bits of dead matter are left over from scavenger meals. Many types of **bacteria** break down these bits. These bacteria are called **decomposers**. All that's left are even tinier bits.

Fact!

Dead animals smell awful. Bacteria break down dead bodies. The smell is created during this process.

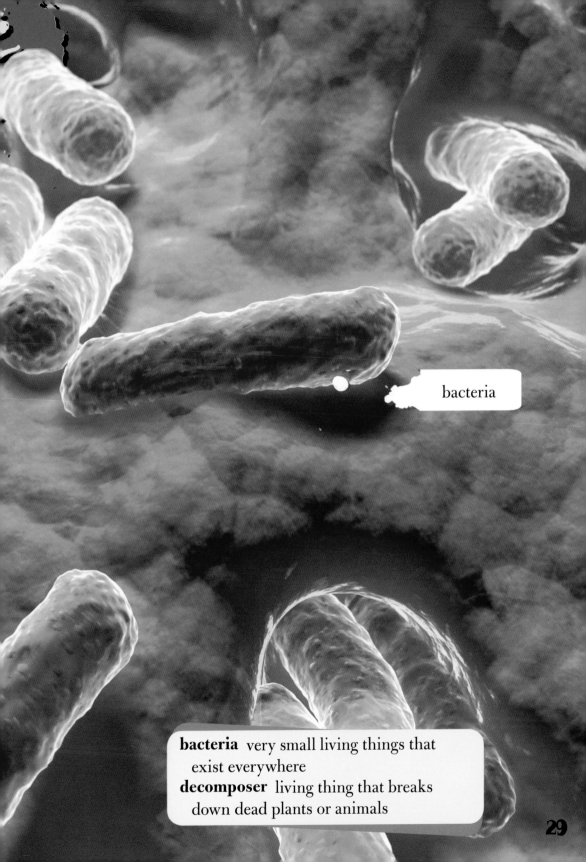

bacteria

bacteria very small living things that
exist everywhere
decomposer living thing that breaks
down dead plants or animals

GLOSSARY

bacteria very small living things that exist everywhere

carcass dead body of an animal

carrion flesh of a dead animal

decomposer living thing that breaks down dead plants or animals

diet what an animal eats

fertilize make soil rich and healthy

larva insect at the stage of development between an egg and an adult

mammal animal with hair or fur that gives birth to young and feeds them milk

nectar sweet liquid found in many flowers

nutrient parts of food, such as vitamins, that are used for growth

omnivore animal that eats plants and other animals

predator animal that hunts other animals for food

scavenger animal that feeds on animals that are already dead

READ MORE

Brilliant Birds (Extreme Animals), Isabel Thomas (Raintree, 2013)

Fearsome Fish (Creatures of the Deep), Rachel Lynette (Raintree, 2012)

Hyena (A Day in the Life: Grassland Animals), Louise Spilsbury (Raintree, 2012)

That's Life, Robert Winston (Dorling Kindersley, 2012)

WEBSITES

www.bbc.co.uk/bigcat/animals/hyenas/hyenas.shtml
How long does it take for a pack of hyenas to eat a zebra?
Find out this answer and more.

**http://kids.nationalgeographic.com/content/kids/
en_US/animals/earthworm/**
Interesting facts and photos. Learn more about the
earthworm.

INDEX